EXPLORING COUNTRIES
Hungary
by Lisa Owings

BELLWETHER MEDIA • MINNEAPOLIS, MN

Note to Librarians, Teachers, and Parents:

Blastoff! Readers are carefully developed by literacy experts and combine standards-based content with developmentally appropriate text.

Level 1 provides the most support through repetition of high-frequency words, light text, predictable sentence patterns, and strong visual support.

Level 2 offers early readers a bit more challenge through varied simple sentences, increased text load, and less repetition of high-frequency words.

Level 3 advances early-fluent readers toward fluency through increased text and concept load, less reliance on visuals, longer sentences, and more literary language.

Level 4 builds reading stamina by providing more text per page, increased use of punctuation, greater variation in sentence patterns, and increasingly challenging vocabulary.

Level 5 encourages children to move from "learning to read" to "reading to learn" by providing even more text, varied writing styles, and less familiar topics.

Whichever book is right for your reader, Blastoff! Readers are the perfect books to build confidence and encourage a love of reading that will last a lifetime!

This edition first published in 2015 by Bellwether Media, Inc.

No part of this publication may be reproduced in whole or in part without written permission of the publisher. For information regarding permission, write to Bellwether Media, Inc., Attention: Permissions Department, 5357 Penn Avenue South, Minneapolis, MN 55419.

Library of Congress Cataloging-in-Publication Data

Owings, Lisa.
  Hungary / by Lisa Owings.
      pages cm. – (Blastoff! Readers: Exploring Countries)
  Includes bibliographical references and index.
  Summary: "Developed by literacy experts for students in grades three through seven, this book introduces young readers to the geography and culture of Hungary"– Provided by publisher.
  Audience: Ages 7-12.
  ISBN 978-1-62617-175-6 (hardcover : alk. paper)
  1. Hungary–Juvenile literature. I. Title.
  DB906.O94 2015
  943.9–dc23
                                                            2014034755

Printed in the United States of America, North Mankato, MN.

Contents

Hungary is a **landlocked** country in central Europe. Seven other countries surround Hungary. Austria lies to the northwest. Across the northern border is Slovakia. A small part of Ukraine touches Hungary in the northeast. Romania shares a long border with Hungary to the southeast. Serbia and Croatia lie to the south and southwest. The last bit of the western border is sealed by Slovenia.

The heart of Hungary is its capital, Budapest. This elegant city is a union of the historic cities Buda and Pest. The two areas are joined by bridges across the **scenic** Danube River. Pest buzzes with activity along the river's eastern bank. Buda stands majestically on the western bank.

Austria

Slovenia

N
W   E
S

Ukraine

Slovakia

Hungary

Budapest

Romania

Danube
River

Serbia

Croatia

Did you know?
Hungary used to be much larger than its
35,918 square miles (93,028 square kilometers).
The country lost more than two-thirds of its land
in a peace agreement after World War I.

Danube River

Hungary is full of low mountains and **fertile** land. In the northwestern corner of the country is the Little Hungarian **Plain**. The Danube River traces the plain's northern border before bending south. A ridge of mountains and green hills crosses Hungary from southwest to northeast. **Volcanoes** formed the tallest peaks.

The Great Hungarian Plain stretches south of the mountains and east of the Danube. Its grasslands are crisscrossed by rivers. The Tisza River is the most important river in eastern Hungary. Its waters support farms during the dry, warm summers. Winters can be bitterly cold, but autumn and spring are beautiful.

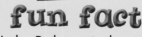

fun fact

Lake Balaton is the largest freshwater lake in central Europe. This long, narrow lake lies in the hills of western Hungary.

Hidden beneath northwestern Hungary are hundreds of beautiful caves. Formed over millions of years, the caves are now part of Aggtelek National Park. Their dark caverns are filled with dangling **stalactites** and towering **stalagmites**. Other cave wonders include delicate **mineral** formations, blue ice curtains, and underground streams.

Aggtelek's Baradla Cave is the largest cave in Hungary. Thousands of years ago, this cave was home to early humans. Today, visitors can spend hours exploring its tall rooms. The walls are covered in formations that look like running water. Rising from the cave floor is Hungary's tallest stalagmite. Visitors are even treated to concerts that echo through the limestone **chambers**.

red deer

Hungarian hills and forests are home to a variety of animals. Red deer and wild boars wander through the forests. The rare wolf or jackal might pose a threat to them. Most other animals in Hungary are small. Rodents scurry over the plains. At night, bats feast on insects.

wild boar

crane

purple emperor butterfly

Hundreds of kinds of birds and butterflies can be spotted in Hungary. People come from all over to admire the thousands of cranes that pass through each fall. Clouds of large copper and purple emperor butterflies are equally stunning. The country's rivers and lakes are full of pike, perch, and other fish. Frogs and toads send up a chorus of chirps at sundown.

Around 10 million people live in Hungary. More than nine out of every ten are Hungarian. Their **ancestors** were **native** to the area. Nearly all of them speak Hungarian, the country's official language. The next-largest group is the Roma, sometimes called Gypsies. Their ancestors came from India and spread throughout the world. Other small groups include Germans and peoples from neighboring countries.

People in Hungary are free to choose their religion. More than half belong to various branches of Christianity. Most others do not follow a specific religion. Hungarians are generally accepting of different beliefs and cultures. At the same time, they are proud of their unique language and history.

Speak Hungarian!

English	Hungarian	How to say it
hello	szia	SEE-ya
good-bye	viszontlátásra	VEE-sont-la-ta-shra
yes	igen	EE-ghen
no	nem	nem
please	kérem	KAY-rem
thank you	köszönöm	KUH-suh-num
friend	barát	buh-RAHT

Budapest

Most Hungarians live in Budapest and other cities. Families usually rent small apartments. To get to work or school, they hop on a bus or train. Some drive cars. For short trips, many prefer to walk or bike. Hungarians in cities can shop at malls, small stores, and markets.

In the countryside, most families live in small houses with tiled roofs. Many have vegetable gardens where they grow some of their own food. Families in the countryside often don't have access to buses and trains. They need cars to get around. Wealthier Hungarians often have a home in the city and a cottage in the countryside.

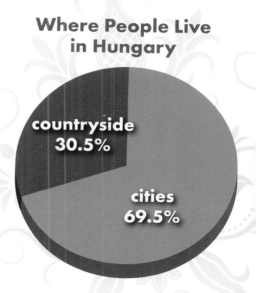

Where People Live in Hungary

countryside 30.5%

cities 69.5%

Did you know?

Hungarian students have a special way of celebrating graduation from primary and secondary school. They march through the halls singing songs and saying good-bye to their teachers and younger students.

Many Hungarian children start preschool before age 5. After that, they go to kindergarten for a year to prepare for school. Between the ages of 6 and 14, children attend primary school. They practice reading and writing in Hungarian. Students also learn history, math, and **foreign** languages. After eight years, they can choose which secondary school to attend.

Some secondary schools offer general classes. They help students prepare for college. Other secondary schools help students learn skills they need for specific jobs. Hungarians who complete four years of general secondary school take a tough exam. If they score well, they can move on to one of many universities in the country.

Where People Work in Hungary

manufacturing 29.7%

farming 7.1%

services 63.2%

More than half of Hungarians have **service jobs**. Some work in banks, schools, or hospitals. Others serve people in hotels and restaurants. They help **tourists** enjoy their stay. Many people in Hungary work in mines or factories. Miners dig up bauxite to be made into aluminum. They also **extract** coal, oil, and natural gas from the earth.

Factory workers make food, paper products, and chemicals. Some produce cars and other machinery. A small number of Hungarians farm the land. Wheat and corn are the most important crops. Farmers also grow sunflower seeds, potatoes, and apples. Some raise cows and other animals for meat or milk.

People in Hungary keep busy with sports and activities. Soccer has the largest number of fans. Hungarians play soccer, watch games on television, and check their team's scores in the newspaper. Lake Balaton is a popular place to gather for swimming, boating, and fishing. People also enjoy hiking through the mountains or riding bicycles or skateboards through city streets.

Friends often meet up at coffee shops or share a meal together. Afterward, they might go to a concert or play. Families enjoy taking day trips to museums or parks. For longer trips, Hungarians like to spend time relaxing at **spa resorts** or sunbathing on Croatian beaches.

Hungarian food is rich and spicy. Many dishes are flavored with the peppery seasoning paprika. *Goulash* is a classic soup of beef, potatoes, onions, and paprika. Spicy fish soup called *halászlé* is also popular. Meat dishes such as paprika chicken are often served with noodles or dumplings. Hungarians also enjoy cabbage leaves or peppers stuffed with meat and rice.

Pancakes and pastries are beloved throughout the country. Thin pancakes called *palacsinta* can have sweet or **savory** fillings. Fried dough topped with sour cream and cheese is a popular snack. Sweet strudels and cakes are often flavored with apples, walnuts, or poppy seeds. Chilled cherry soup is a favorite summer treat.

goulash

halászlé

fun fact
Chimney cakes are made by wrapping dough around a wooden handle and cooking it over a fire. The chimney-shaped treats are rolled in sugar before being pulled apart and eaten.

Easter and Christmas are the major religious holidays in Hungary. Springtime Easter celebrations include decorating eggs and feasting on ham. On December 5, children leave their shoes out overnight for St. Nicholas. They wake on St. Nicholas Day to find them filled with treats. On Christmas Eve, families gather to decorate trees, share a special meal, and attend church. Christmas on December 25 is for relaxing and visiting.

A national holiday on March 15 celebrates Hungary's fight for independence from Austria. People wear national colors and gather for **ceremonies** and speeches. St. Stephen's Day on August 20 honors the first king of Hungary. Hungarians celebrate with music, dancing, and fireworks.

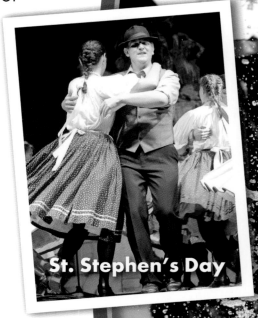
St. Stephen's Day

Did you know?
At Easter, it is tradition in some places for boys to throw water on girls. The girls represent flowers.

Buda

Castle Hill

Facing each other across the Danube River stand the two distinct historic cities of Buda and Pest. Quiet Buda was once home to Hungarian royalty. At its heart is Castle Hill, topped by the royal palace's copper dome. Today the castle houses a museum, art gallery, and library. The hilltop views are as grand as its royal history.

Pest

parliament
building

Unlike its neighbor, Pest is busy and modern. Gleaming shops and restaurants line its bustling streets. Hungary's government is also located in Pest. The famous **parliament** building was finished in 1902. Its **ornate** white arches and steep **turrets** mimic **Gothic** architecture. Buda and Pest joined in 1873. The united cities represent Hungary's past and present and the **traditional** yet modern values of its people.

Fast Facts About Hungary

Hungary's Flag

The Hungarian flag has three horizontal bands of red, white, and green. The colors come from the national coat of arms. Red stands for fierce battles, white for freedom, and green for fertile land. Hungary's flag was adopted in 1957.

Official Name: Hungary

Area: 35,918 square miles (93,028 square kilometers); Hungary is the 110th largest country in the world.

Capital City:	Budapest
Important Cities:	Debrecen, Miskolc, Szeged
Population:	9,919,128 (July 2014)
Official Language:	Hungarian
National Holiday:	St. Stephen's Day (August 20)
Religions:	Christian (52.8%), other (1.9%), none (18.2%), unspecified (27.1%)
Major Industries:	services, tourism, manufacturing, farming, mining
Natural Resources:	bauxite, coal, natural gas, oil
Manufactured Products:	metals, food products, wood and paper products, clothing, chemicals, vehicles
Farm Products:	wheat, corn, sunflower seeds, potatoes, apples, grapes, livestock
Unit of Money:	forint; the forint is divided into 100 fillér.

Glossary

ancestors—relatives who lived long ago

ceremonies—formal events that mark important occasions

chambers—rooms or enclosed spaces

extract—to remove something by pulling it out

fertile—able to support growth

foreign—from or relating to a different nation

Gothic—a style of architecture known for its pointed arches, tall towers, and large windows

landlocked—completely surrounded by land

mineral—a substance naturally formed in the earth

native—originally from a specific place

ornate—covered with decorations

parliament—the group of lawmakers for some governments

plain—a large area of flat land

savory—spicy or salty, not sweet

scenic—having beautiful natural surroundings

service jobs—jobs that perform tasks for people or businesses

spa resorts—places, often with natural hot springs, where people go to relax and improve their health

stalactites—icicle-shaped formations that hang from the roof of a cave

stalagmites—column-shaped formations that rise from the floor of a cave

tourists—people who travel to visit another place

traditional—related to a custom, idea, or belief handed down from one generation to the next

turrets—small towers on a building

volcanoes—holes in the earth; when a volcano erupts, hot, melted rock called lava shoots out.

To Learn More

AT THE LIBRARY

Guillain, Charlotte. *Hungary*. Chicago, Ill.: Heinemann Library, 2012.

Hargittai, Magdolna. *Cooking the Hungarian Way: Revised and Expanded to Include New Low-Fat and Vegetarian Recipes*. Minneapolis, Minn.: Lerner Publications Co., 2003.

Molnár, Irma. *One-Time Dog Market at Buda and Other Hungarian Folktales*. North Haven, Conn.: Linnet Books, 2001.

ON THE WEB

Learning more about Hungary is as easy as 1, 2, 3.

1. Go to www.factsurfer.com.

2. Enter "Hungary" into the search box.

3. Click the "Surf" button and you will see a list of related web sites.

With factsurfer.com, finding more information is just a click away.

Index